First published in 2005 by Prufrock Press Inc.

Published in 2016 by Routledge
605 Third Avenue, New York, NY 10017
2 Park Square, Milton Park, Abingdon, Oxon OX14 4RN

Routledge is an imprint of the Taylor & Francis Group, an informa business

ISBN: 9781593630911 (pbk)

DOI: 10.4324/9781003236306

Contents

Information for the Instructor

Pack your gear and get ready to take your students on a safari. But on this safari, you won't be stalking wild animals. You'll be stalking clues that you can piece together to solve deductive logic puzzles. The reward for this expedition will be a bounty of thinking skills. *Logic Safari* gives students an opportunity to sort through related bits of information by combining, relating, ordering, and eliminating. The result is the logical linking together of ideas that leads to the puzzle's solution.

Each puzzle in *Logic Safari* has three parts. These parts are:
1. **The introduction** - This paragraph sets the background and helps students become familiar with the elements of the puzzle.
2. **The clues** - The clues relate all of the components and provide a basis for the logical linking together of the pieces of information, thereby allowing students to make deductions that will lead to the solution.
3. **The grid** - The grid provides a worksheet for sorting, eliminating and associating the clues. Every square on the grid represents a possible answer. By eliminating possibilities, one is finally left with only one choice per row or column. The one square that is not been eliminated is one correct solution. When this is done for every row and column, the puzzle solution is complete.

Any marking system for the grid is valid if it is used consistently. Many students prefer to use an **X** in a square to represent elimination of a choice and an **O** to represent a correct answer. Using "yes" and "no" works equally well.

In addition to these three parts, students may wish to jot down notes on scratch paper. This may help them in putting the information in rank order or in visualizing the relationships. It should be stressed that there is always more than one way to correctly solve a puzzle; and in sharing the way in which each person used the clues to arrive at the solution, students will gain insights into different modes of thinking.

Students will find that it is necessary to look not only at each clue individually, but also to look at the clues in relation to one another in order to derive as much information as possible. For example, if the clues state, "Gina is older than Eric and the girl with the teddy bear but younger than Gonzales," we can deduce a lot of information by the proper arrangement of the clues. If there four people in the puzzle, we know that Gina is second in rank of age. If there are two boys and two girls, we also know that Gonzales is a boy. We can also deduce that Mary is not Gonzales, Eric is not Gonzales, Gonzales does not have a teddy bear, Gina does not have a teddy bear, and Eric does not have a teddy bear. In addition, we know that Gonzales is the oldest. With one clue, then we have been able to make several eliminations and two positive connections.

There are three books in this series, so students are able to move from easy to intermediate levels of difficulty in deductive thinking. *Logic Safari* puzzles are an excellent way to strengthen students' logical deductive thinking skills. Students find the puzzles very motivating, and as they work with these puzzles they grow in their abilities to sort through information and make connections.

Yearbook

Marilyn, Linda, Elizabeth and Jonah are doing photography, layout, captions and sales for their yearbook. Their deadlines are December 20, January 20, February 1 and February 15. Sort through these clues to determine who does what job and when the task must be completed.

Clues

1. Elizabeth's deadline is before the girl in charge of sales and the girl who is doing captions but after the boy who is the photographer.

2. Marilyn has a later deadline than the girl doing the captions.

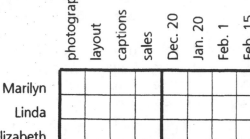

	photography	layout	captions	sales	Dec. 20	Jan. 20	Feb. 1	Feb. 15
Marilyn								
Linda								
Elizabeth								
Jonah								
Dec. 20				
Jan. 20				
Feb. 1				
Feb. 15				

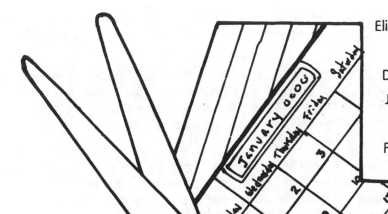

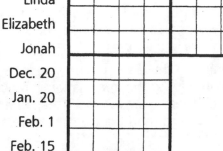

Camp Out

Cole, Lance, John and Jay are camping out. Each has a special dish that they are preparing on the campfire, and each has a minor injury that is a nuisance. Set up camp with these clues to determine what each camper will cook and what injury each has experienced.

Clues

1. The boy who can make cobbler over a campfire, the boy who got sunburned, the boy who fixes corn on the cob, and Cole planned for this camp out for weeks.

2. The boy who prepares foil-fried potatoes, the boy pestered by chiggers, John and Lance all know about safety in the outdoors.

3. The boy who fixes the cobbler, the boy who can cook trout, and Jay tried to help their friend with his poison ivy.

4. Lance does not have briar scratches because he did not need to pick blackberries for the cobbler.

5. Cole does not fix the trout.

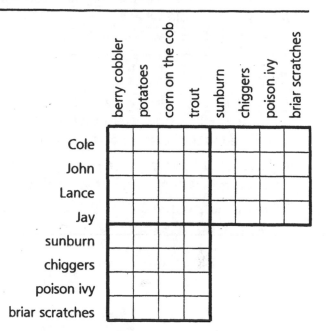

Miniature Golf

Travis, Sandra, Rich and Kate just finished playing miniature golf. Each player scored a hole-in-one at either the waterfall hole, the windmill, the kangaroo hole, or the hole with a drawbridge and a castle. Their final scores were 72, 75, 80 and 82. Tee off with these clues to determine who did what.

Note: In golf the lower score is the better.

Clues

1. Kate, the boy who shot the hole-in-one on the hole featuring a giant kangaroo, the girl who got her hole-in-one after putting between the revolving blades of a windmill, and the boy who finished with the score of 72 all enjoy outdoor recreation.

2. Sandra got a better score than Travis and the girl who got a hole-in-one by the waterfall, but her score was not as good as Rich's score.

3. Travis had a better score than Kate but had more putts than the girl with a hole-in-one by the windmill and the boy who got his hole-in-one by the castle.

Parent Volunteers

Mrs Shields, Mr. Costello, Mrs. Maxwell and Mrs. Hoehn are volunteers at Claymont School. They are the parents of Ed, Rachel, Drew and Terrence. They volunteer on Monday, Tuesday, Thursday or Friday and work in the library, with the art appreciation project, as a math tutor or by helping the nurse. Use these clues to determine which parent does what.

Clues

1. Mrs. Shields, the lady who helps in the library, Rachel's dad, and the lady who works as a math tutor all feel they provide a valuable service to the school.

2. Mrs. Maxwell, the lady who helps in the nurse's office, Drew's mom, and the person who does art appreciation on Fridays have all received recognition for their help.

3. Ed's mom works later in the week than the lady in the library and Mrs. Hoehn, but she works earlier in the week than Mr. Costello.

4. Mrs. Maxwell can't volunteer on Monday or Thursday.

Lemonade Stand

Alex, Zack, Manuel and Anna decided to have a lemonade stand. Each furnished either the lemons, sugar, cherries or ice. Each provided either the pitchers, glasses, coolers or the table. Each had a special job — making signs, washing glasses, serving customers or making change. Squeeze out these clues to determine who did what at the lemonade stand.

Clues

1. The boy who provided lemons, the boy furnished the coolers and ice, the girl who served customers, and Alex all live on Glenwood Drive.

2. The boy who supplied the table and the cherries also made change.

3. The boy who brought the lemons, the girl who provided the sugar, the boy with the coolers, and the boy who made change all agreed to share the profits equally.

4. Zack had to go home to get more ice.

5. Zack did not wash glasses.

6. Anna did not furnish the pitchers.

Homecoming Parade

Martin, Peg, Frank and Yvonne are in the homecoming parade. They are in the bicycle brigade, the queen's court float, the marching band and the football float. They are in the 9th, 10th, 11th and 12th grades, and they are either the second, fifth, sixth or twelfth entry in the parade. March through these clues to determine what each student is doing in the parade.

Clues

1. Martin is nearer the beginning of the parade than the girl riding on the queen's court float and the boy on the football float, but he comes after Yvonne.

2. Frank is in a higher grade than the girl with the marching band and Peg, but he is in a lower grade than the boy who is with the fifth entry.

3. The person with the queen's court is in a higher grade than the girl with the marching band.

4. The queen's court float is the final parade feature.

	bicycle brigade	queen's court	marching band	football float	9th grade	10th grade	11th grade	12th grade	2nd entry	5th entry	6th entry	12th entry
Martin												
Peg												
Frank												
Yvonne												
2nd entry												
5th entry												
6th entry												
12th entry												
9th grade												
10th grade												
11th grade												
12th grade												

Fish Fry

Jane, Amanda, Blake and Sue attended the last fish fry of the season in their community. Each loves a different variety of fish, made a different accompanying dish, and supplied some type of equipment needed to make the fish fry a success. Flip through these clues to determine who did what.

Clues

1. Jane, the boy who made cole slaw, the girl who loves catfish, and the girl who brought chairs for people to sit on all rode on Blake's father's hay wagon from the highway to the banks of Pigeon Creek.

2. Sue, the boy who only eats trout, the girl who supplied plates, and the girl who brought tablecloths all helped spread the news of the fish fry throughout the community.

3. Blake, the girl who prefers bass, the girl who baked three dozen apple dumplings, and Amanda waded in Pigeon Creek.

4. Jane does not eat bluegill or catfish.

5. Amanda, and the girl who made the hush puppies, and the girl supplying chairs all helped catch the fish.

6. Sue does not like catfish.

7. Jane did not supply the plates.

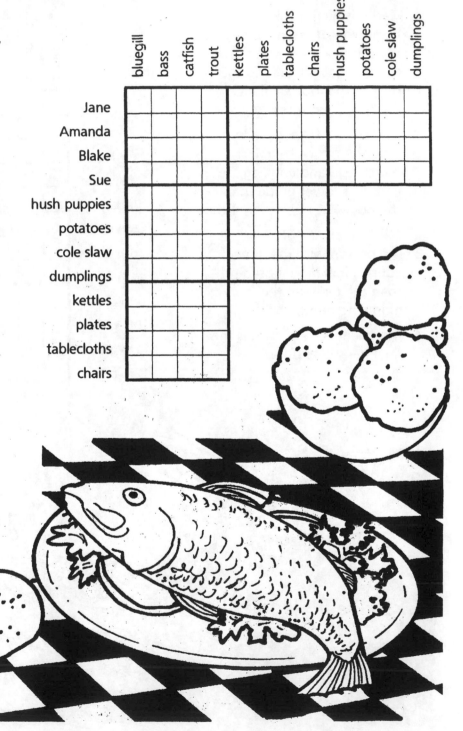

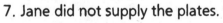

© Taylor & Francis Groups • *Logic Safari, Book 3*

Animal Crackers

Chad, Christina, Cassandra, Sam, Christopher and Molly were baking animal crackers in the shapes of elephants, bears, lions, fish, chickens and cows. They baked 24, 28, 32, 36, 38 and 42 of the different shapes. Crack open these clues to determine who baked what kind of cookies.

Clues

1. Chad made more cookies than the girl making elephants, the boy making lions and Cassandra, but he made fewer than the girl making fish and Christopher.

2. The boy baking cows made six more cookies than the boy cutting out bears and four more than Christina.

3. There were more elephants than lions but fewer elephants than chickens.

	elephants	bears	lions	fish	chickens	cows	24 cookies	28 cookies	32 cookies	36 cookies	38 cookies	42 cookies
Chad												
Christina												
Cassandra												
Sam												
Christopher												
Molly												
24 cookies						
28 cookies						
32 cookies						
36 cookies						
38 cookies						
42 cookies						

Trivia Contest

Forrest, Debra, Gene and Vicky are students in the sixth, seventh and eighth grades who are taking part in a trivia contest to raise funds to help preserve the rain forests. Each student has one strong category (television, movies, history, sports), each has earned a certain number of points (392, 380, 368, 325), and each has pledges from a certain number of people (45, 40, 30, 25) to donate money for each point the participant scores. Sort through these clues to match each student with the correct category, grade, points and number of sponsors.

Clues

1. Forrest, the two girls in the eighth grade, and the boy who knows a lot about sports trivia are all concerned about saving the rain forests.

2. Debra has scored more points than the boy whose strong category is history and the boy who has found 45 pledges but fewer than the girl who is a whiz at television trivia.

3. The seventh grader has scored more points than the boy with 40 pledges.

4. Vicky has more pledges than the movie trivia expert but fewer than the sixth grader and Gene.

Apple Orchard Hay Ride

Gail, Eric, Tami and Greg went to a local orchard to pick apples. The four friends rode on the same hay wagon into the orchards but got off at various locations in order to pick Jonathan, golden delicious, red delicious and winesap apples. They picked 2 pecks, 3 pecks, 1 bushel and 11/2 bushels before riding different wagons back to the harvest barn where they paid for their apples and purchased apple cider, apple butter and an apple pie. Pick through these clues to determine who did what.   Note: 4 pecks = 1 bushel

Clues

1. Gail, the boy who picked golden delicious, the girl who picked 3 pecks, and the boy who purchased a gigantic apple pie all sampled apples fresh from the tree.

2. Eric, the girl who picked Jonathans, the girl with red delicious, and the boy who picked winesaps enjoyed the beautiful autumn weather while foraging within the many acres of orchards.

3. Tami arrived back at the harvest barn before Greg and the girl who purchased a gallon of cider but after the boy who bought cider.

4. Gail arrived at the harvest barn after the boy with golden delicious apples and the girl picking 3 pecks but before the boy buying 2 pecks.

5. Gail picked more apples than the girl gathering red delicious and the boy who picked golden delicious.

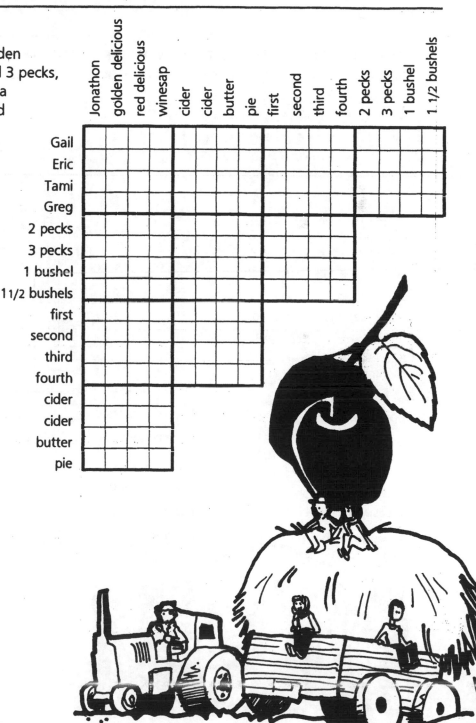

Copy Cats

Kate, Carlos, Jack, Craig, Neal and Daniel imitated famous Americans from history for Copy Cat Day. They impersonated George Washington, Benjamin Franklin, Betsy Ross, Thomas Jefferson, Abraham Lincoln and John Hancock. Each student was correctly identified by 4, 5, 7, 8, 9 and 10 of their classmates. Sort through these clues to determine who impersonated which famous person and how many classmates were able to guess their identity.

Clues

1. Kate, the boy posing as George Washington, the boy impersonating Benjamin Franklin, the boy dressed as Thomas Jefferson, the boy who was Abraham Lincoln, and the boy copying John Hancock all researched their characters very carefully.

2. More students guessed who Jack was impersonating than the boy doing John Hancock, the boy doing Lincoln, or Neal or Daniel, but Jack had fewer correct guesses than Kate.

3. Carlos and Jack were not Washington or Franklin and did not receive 4, 5, or 7 correct guesses from their classmates.

4. Lincoln received more correct guesses than Craig, Neal, or the boy posing as Washington.

5. The boy impersonating George Washington received more guesses than the person dressed as Benjamin Franklin but fewer guesses than the student impersonating John Hancock.

	George Washington	Benjamin Franklin	Betsy Ross	Thomas Jefferson	Abraham Lincoln	John Hancock	4 correct guesses	5 correct guesses	7 correct guesses	8 correct guesses	9 correct guesses	10 correct guesses
Kate												
Carlos												
Jack												
Craig												
Neal												
Daniel												
4 correct guesses												
5 correct guesses												
7 correct guesses												
8 correct guesses												
9 correct guesses												
10 correct guesses												

Team Pictures

Kevin, Jeff, Doug and Paul, whose coaches are Hersey, Olson, Reynolds and Tate, are having their team pictures taken today at 12:30, 1:00, 1:15 and 1:45 p.m. Their team names are the Bobcats, the Cardinals, the Cougars and the Tornadoes. Their uniforms are red, blue, gray, and maroon. Line up these clues to determine which boy belongs to which team, wears which colors, and when he will get his picture taken.

Clues

1. Kevin's team gets their picture taken before Coach Tate's team but after the Bobcats and the team wearing maroon.

2. Doug's team gets their picture taken after Coach Hersey's team but before the Tornadoes or the team wearing red.

3. Jeff, the boy on Olson's team, the boy with the Bobcats, and the boy in maroon all play first base.

4. Paul will get his picture taken before the Bobcats, before Coach Olson's Tornadoes, and before Jeff's team that wears red.

5. The Cardinals are wearing red and the Bobcats have gray uniforms.

Natural Disaster Kits

Mr. Smith, Mrs. Wilson, Mr. Hiatt, Mrs. Althoff, Mr. Detwiler and Mrs. Horowitz have volunteered to prepare natural disaster kits for all the classrooms and keep them up to date with distilled water, flashlights, food, radios, batteries and first aid supplies. Each of these people has one child in either 1st, 2nd, 3rd, 4th, 5th or 6th grade. Test out these clues to determine what each person's contribution will be.

Clues

1. The woman in charge of distilled water, the man with a 3rd grader, the woman with a 2nd grader, the lady supplying batteries, Mr. Smith, and Mr. Detwiler all take their jobs seriously.

2. The woman supplying flashlights has a child in a lower grade than the man in charge of food, the woman with distilled water, the man doing first aid supplies, and the man in charge of radios, but her child is in a higher grade than Mrs. Horowitz's child.

3. The woman with the 1st grader, the woman supplying flashlights, and Mrs. Wilson all live within two blocks of the school.

4. Mr. Smith's daughter is two grades ahead of the son of the man in charge of the first aid supplies.

5. Mr. Smith is not in charge of the food.

6. Mr. Detwiler is not in charge of the first aid supplies.

7. Mr. Detwiler's son is not in the fourth or fifth grades.

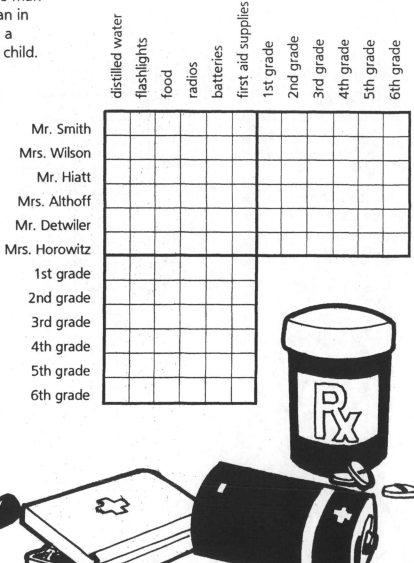

Student of the Week Awards

Justin, Maria, Nicholas and Danielle have been awarded Student of the Week awards. Each person has a different last name, and each was nominated by a different teacher (Mrs. Buck, Mrs. Kinney, Mrs. Horstmann and Mrs. Maloney). They received either a certificate, a bumper sticker, a button or lunch with the principal. Each one earned the title at different times between the first week of October and the second week of February. Study the clues to discover the facts about these special students.

Clues

1. Justin and Barton both received the award during the same month.

2. Mrs. Buck and Mrs. Kinney nominated girls.

3. The boy who won the bumper sticker and Nicholas were proud that their pictures were displayed on the bulletin board.

4. Barton was honored by having lunch with the principal because this was his fourth nomination.

5. The girl nominated by Mrs. Kinney, the girl honored the second week in February, the boy honored the third week of October, and Adams all posed for a yearbook picture.

6. Maria received her certificate before Christmas break.

7. Justin was not nominated by Mrs. Horstmann.

8. Chang received the award on Lincoln's birthday.

	Barton	Adams	Chang	Sousa	1st week of Oct.	3rd week of Oct.	1st week of Dec.	2nd week of Feb.	certificate	bumper sticker	button	lunch	Mrs. Buck	Mrs. Kinney	Mrs. Horstmann	Mrs. Maloney
Justin																
Maria																
Nicholas																
Danielle																
Mrs. Buck																
Mrs. Kinney																
Mrs. Horstmann																
Mrs. Maloney																
certificate																
bumper sticker																
button																
lunch																
1st week of Oct.																
3rd week of Oct.																
1st week of Dec.																
2nd week of Feb.																

Tyler's Birthday

Some special people (Grandma, Grandpa, Aunt Amy, Uncle Randy, Aunt Bonnie, Cousin Becky, and Mom and Dad) came to Tyler's first birthday. They brought gifts (a push glowworm, a squeeze light-up toy, a bubble machine, a rocking horse, sidewalk chalk, and a foam bat and ball) and food. Unwrap these clues to determine who brought what to Tyler's party.

Clues

1. Grandma and Grandpa arrived ahead of the aunt who brought the bubble machine, the aunt who brought the gelatin salad, the uncle with the vegetable tray, and the person who brought sidewalk chalk.

2. Mom and Dad gave Tyler his rocking horse before the guests arrived.

3. Mom made Tyler's cake, and Grandma always brings her famous potato salad to family get-togethers.

4. The bat and ball was not from a woman.

5. The person with the sidewalk chalk did not make the deviled eggs.

6. The aunt with the squeeze toy and the aunt with the deviled eggs came together.

7. Tyler's grandparents gave him a push toy.

8. Aunt Bonnie did not bring deviled eggs.

	push glowworm	squeeze toy	bubble machine	rocking horse	sidewalk chalk	bat and ball	potato salad	vegetable tray	gelatin salad	deviled eggs	birthday cake	barbecued meat
Grandma and Grandpa												
Aunt Amy												
Uncle Randy												
Aunt Bonnie												
Cousin Becky												
Mom and Dad												
potato salad												
vegetable tray												
gelatin salad												
deviled eggs												
birthday cake												
barbecued meat												

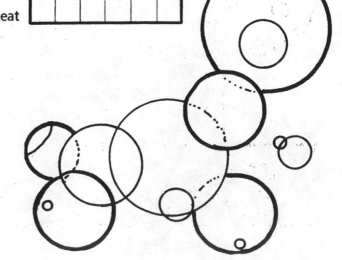

Water Balloon Fight

Andrew, Brent, Matt and Ted, whose partners are Todd, Miguel, Casey and Jose, are having a water balloon fight using red, yellow, blue and orange balloons. Their bases are the patio table, the front porch, the wheelbarrow and the garden. The pairs of boys have 40, 38, 35 and 34 balloons. Burst open these clues to find out about this wet entertainment.

Clues

1. The boy whose partner is Casey, the boy using the wheelbarrow, the boy using red balloons, and Andrew are good friends.

2. Brent and his partner have more balloons than the boy with Todd and the boy whose base is the garden, but they have fewer than Matt.

3. Jose's partner has the most balloons and stores them in the wheelbarrow.

4. There are four more orange balloons than red ones.

5. Miguel is not Andrew's or Brent's partner.

6. There are more yellow balloons than blue ones.

7. The patio table holds blue balloons.

	Todd	Miguel	Casey	Jose	40 balloons	38 balloons	35 balloons	34 balloons	red	yellow	blue	orange	patio table	front porch	wheelbarrow	garden
Andrew																
Brent																
Matt																
Ted																
patio table																
front porch																
wheelbarrow																
garden																
red																
yellow																
blue																
orange																
40 balloons																
38 balloons																
35 balloons																
34 balloons																

Family Garden

Robert has a beautiful garden of flowers that have been passed down from his ancestors. Six different kinds of flowers have been handed down from Great Grandma Frona, Great Grandma Pearl, Grandma Maxine, Grandma Mary, Grandpa Jack, and Great Aunt Kitty. The flowers have been propagated by cuttings, seeds, bulbs, rhizomes, and roots. Prune through these clues to determine each flower's origin.

Clues

1. The rose has been handed down at least six generations and the cuttings have gone to many descendants.

2. Grandma Maxine contributed the poppies.

3. The two great grandmothers' flowers came from rhizomes and cuttings.

4. The man who contributed the peonies is as skilled at gardening as his wife, whose flowers started from seeds, and his mother, who gave Robert the rose, and his sister, who contributed the hollyhocks.

5. The poppy seeds are much smaller than seeds collected from the hollyhocks.

6. Great Grandma Pearl's flowers grow from rhizomes.

7. Mary's flowers grow from bulbs, and she is not married to Jack.

8. Irises grow from rhizomes.

	poppies	roses	irises	tiger lilies	hollyhocks	peonies	cuttings	seeds	seeds	bulbs	rhizomes	roots
Great Grandma Frona												
Great Grandma Pearl												
Grandma Maxine												
Grandma Mary												
Grandpa Jack												
Great Aunt Kitty												
cuttings												
seeds												
seeds												
bulbs												
rhizomes												
roots												

Golf Lessons

Joseph, Roberto, Rick and Jenny are taking golf lessons to work on their chipping, putting, driving and ability to get out of sand traps. Their lessons are at 10:30 a.m., 12:00 noon, 1:30 p.m. and 2:15 p.m. Their instructors are Lee or Charlie and they take the lessons at Deer Meadows Country Club or Beaver Creek Golf Club. Tee up these clues to find out about each person's lesson.

Clues

1. The boy whose lesson is at 10:30 a.m., the boy working on chipping, the girl taking a lesson from Charlie, and Joseph are serious about improving their game.

2. Roberto's lesson is before the boy who is putting, but it is after the boy working on getting out of sand traps and the girl whose lesson is at 12:00 noon.

3. Lee teaches only at Deer Meadows, and Charlie teaches only at Beaver Creek.

4. Joseph and Roberto take lessons from the same pro.

Pine Wood Derby

Robby, Adam, Mike and Nathan participated in the Cub Scout pine wood derby, winning gold, silver and bronze medals and a blue ribbon. The scouts belonged to different dens and were racing in heats at different times. The boys also had different den leaders. Race through these clues to find out about these prize-winning cub scouts.

Clues

1. The boy who won a silver medal, the boy who raced at 11:30 a.m., the boy in Mrs. Rose's den, and Robby all knew one another.

2. The boy in den 7, the boy in den 4, the boy who raced at 12:45 p.m., and Adam all spent many hours crafting their racers.

3. Mike raced after the boy who won a blue ribbon but before the boy winning a silver medal and the boy with the gold medal.

4. Nathan raced after the boy with the blue ribbon, the boy in Mrs. Liming's den, and the boy in Mrs. Barnes' den.

5. Adam raced after the boy in den 7 and the boy winning a bronze medal but before the boy from den 9.

6. Robby did not win a gold medal and was not in Mrs. Liming's or Mrs. Barnes' den.

7. Mrs. Liming was the leader of den 2.

8. The boy racing at 12:15 p.m. won the silver medal.

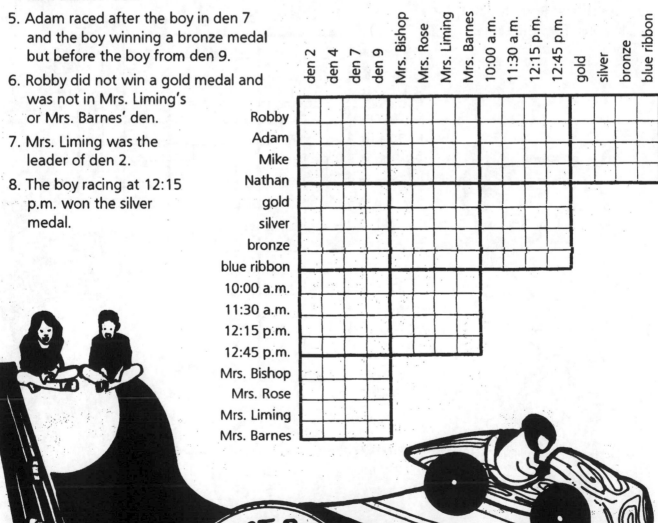

Secretaries' Day

Gwen, Nate, Geneva and Karen are secretaries for Dr. Yoshioka, Ms. Drewes, Mr. Risby and Dr. Waite. They each work in a different kind of office, and each received a different gift for Secretaries' Day. Each was also taken to lunch at either a Mexican, Italian, vegetarian or seafood restaurant. File through these clues to determine where each person works and how they celebrated their special day.

Clues

1. The man who is a secretary for Dr. Yoshioka, the woman who received chocolates, the woman who works in real estate, and Gwen all work in the River Port Plaza.

2. The woman who was taken to the Mexican restaurant and the woman who was taken to the vegetarian restaurant both received flowers.

3. The woman who received chocolates, the woman who works for Ms. Drewes, the woman with Dr. Waite, and the man who is the secretary for the counseling center were all happy about the special attention they received.

4. Ms. Drewes is in real estate, and Mr. Risby runs an insurance agency.

5. Karen did not receive flowers or go to a Mexican restaurant.

6. Mr. Risby is allergic to seafood.

7. Dr. Waite has a medical office.

8. Geneva does not like Mexican food.

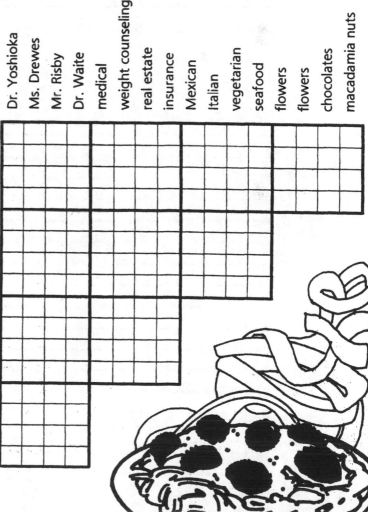

Kittens

Tonia has four kittens (Boots, Bear, Suzy and Sugar) that are all different colors. Two kittens are male and two are female, and they each enjoy a favorite toy. Each kitten has a favorite napping place, and the kittens are different ages. Scratch your way through these clues to determine which kitten is which.

Clues

1. The male cat that is orange, the female cat that loves chasing the jingle ball, the female cat that naps on the daybed, and Boots all get along well.

2. Suzy and her brother are older than the male kitten that chases the toy mouse but younger than Sugar.

3. The kitten that loves the jingle ball, the youngest kitten who hides under the recliner, the male kitten who likes playing with the ribbon and Sugar all play tag with one another.

4. Bear and Suzy are not related.

5. The white cat is the oldest and loves to lie on the daybed.

6. The black and white kitten is a female and loves napping on a kitchen chair.

© Taylor & Francis Groups • *Logic Safari, Book 3*

Garage Sale

Peter, Cindy, David, Jane and Kathy had a garage sale where they earned different amounts of money selling sports equipment, toys, books, clothing and baseball cards. To make bookkeeping simple they each used a different colored price sticker. Rummage through these clues to find out the details of this joint endeavor.

Clues

1. Cindy made more money than the girl who sold toys and the girl who used white stickers but less than the boy selling sports equipment or Peter.

2. Jane made more than the girl selling toys but less than the girl using yellow stickers, David, or the boy using green stickers.

3. The sports equipment brought in $6.00 more than the baseball cards and $11.00 more than the clothes.

4. The sports equipment was priced with blue stickers.

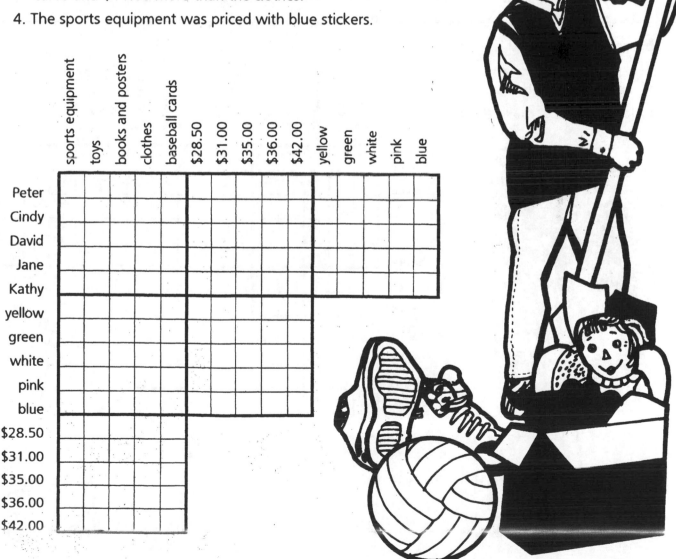

Mother's Day

Heather, Jessica, Joanne, April and Sherita are the daughters of Mrs. Avery, Mrs. Cobb, Mrs. Deutsch, Mrs. Wingrove and Mrs. Yamada. On Mother's Day each girl honored her mother with a special gift and a special treat. Use these clues to determine how each girl honored her mother on Mother's Day.

Clues

1. Mrs. Avery's daughter, the girl who made the card, the girl who gave the dinner, and Heather all think they have very special moms.

2. Mrs. Cobb's daughter, who is friends with April, Jessica, and Joanne finally decided on the sleep shirt as a gift.

3. Sherita bought the concert tickets while her friend April purchased a gift certificate for a manicure.

4. Mrs. Wingrove's daughter surprised her with breakfast in bed and a bouquet.

5. Mrs. Deutsch's daughter made a beautiful card and later gave her a massage.

6. Mrs. Yamada loved her rose bush.

7. Heather fixed fresh melon and blueberry muffins.

8. Joanne did not make a card.

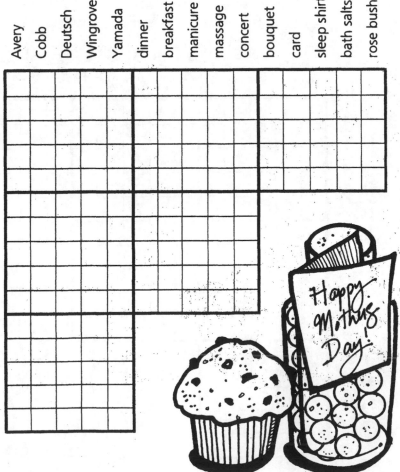

April Creek Walk

Pamela, Vernon, Sean, Tiffany and Shana whose last names are Ho, Lewandowski, O'Brien, Rubin and Walker took a hike down Fox Creek one afternoon in April. Each person spotted one animal and one plant specimen as they enjoyed their springtime walk. Meander through these clues to determine who discovered what on the walk.

Clues

1. The girl who spotted the box turtle, the girl who found the buttercup, Pamela, Ho, and Sean all live somewhere along Fox Creek.

2. Mr. O'Brien told his daughter, Pamela, and Shana to walk carefully and watch for any dangers along the creek bank.

3. The boy spying the garter snake, the girl finding the tree frog, the boy spotting the chipmunk, Rubin, and Shana thoroughly enjoyed their hike.

4. The girl who found the morel, the boy finding the fern, the girl who spotted the buttercup, Vernon, and Shana try to keep Fox Creek unpolluted and free of litter.

5. Lewandowski took pictures of his snake.

6. Walker did not find the mayapples.

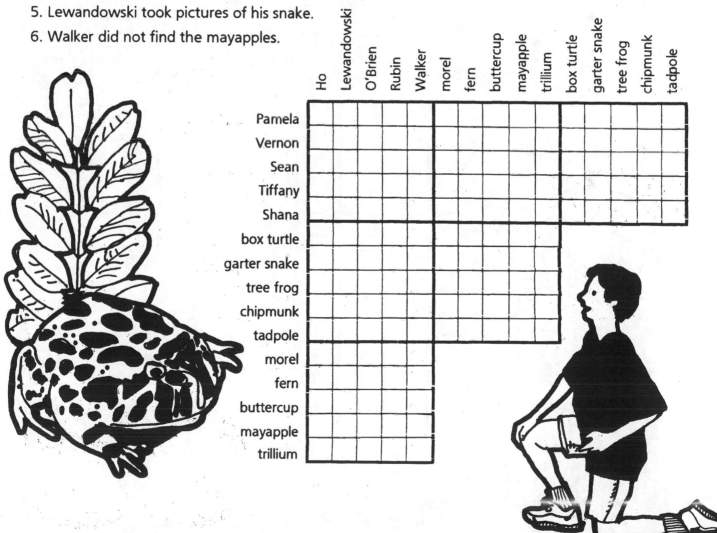

School Carnival

Leah, Kenneth, Troy, Tasha, Darren and Jenna are helping their parents (Mrs. Fishman, Mr. Gonzalez, Mrs. Hollinger, Mr. Lomax, Mrs. Nixon and Mr. Sarni) during various shifts at the school carnival. They are all assisting in different booths. Take a shot at these clues to determine who helps where and at what time.

Clues

1. Leah met her dad at the ring toss before the girl helping her mom at the fish pond, the boy helping his mom at face painting, the girl helping her dad at the lollipop tree, and the boy helping his mom with snow cones but after the boy who helped his dad at the hot dog stand.

2. Kenneth helped Mrs. Fishman two hours after his friend Darren worked.

3. Mr. Gonzalez worked before Kenneth, the boy who helped make snow cones, the girl who helped at the lollipop tree, and Tasha.

4. Mr. Lomax and Darren were the only father-son duo.

5. Mrs. Hollinger worked before Troy but after Mr. Sarni.

	fish pond	ring toss	face painting	lollipop tree	snow cones	hot dogs	Mrs. Fishman	Mr. Gonzalez	Mrs. Hollinger	Mr. Lomax	Mrs. Nixon	Mr. Sarni	8:30-9:30	9:30-10:30	10:30-11:30	11:30-12:30	12:30-1:30	1:30-2:30
Leah																		
Kenneth																		
Troy																		
Tasha																		
Darren																		
Jenna																		
8:30-9:30																		
9:30-10:30																		
10:30-11:30																		
11:30-12:30																		
12:30-1:30																		
1:30-2:30																		
Mrs. Fishman																		
Mr. Gonzalez																		
Mrs. Hollinger																		
Mr. Lomax																		
Mrs. Nixon																		
Mr. Sarni																		

The Card Shop

Crystal, Andy, Laura, Emily, Nadia and Brandon went to the card shop. They each bought a different kind of card that came with different colored envelopes. They paid in cash, by credit card, check, or travelers' check. Unseal these clues to determine who bought what.

Clues

1. The girl who bought an anniversary card and the girl who bought a card with a blue envelope both paid cash.

2. The girl who bought a birthday card, the girl who had a yellow envelope, the boy who got a thank you card, the girl who paid by travelers' check, Crystal, and Andy all came into the shop within 45 minutes of one another.

3. The new baby card came with a blue envelope, the sympathy card with lavender, the anniversary card with yellow, the graduation card with green, the birthday card with pink, and the thank you card with a white envelope.

4. Andy and Nadia used credit cards to get birthday and graduation cards.

5. Laura, Emily, and the girl with the blue envelope checked out right behind one another.

6. Laura's card had a yellow envelope.

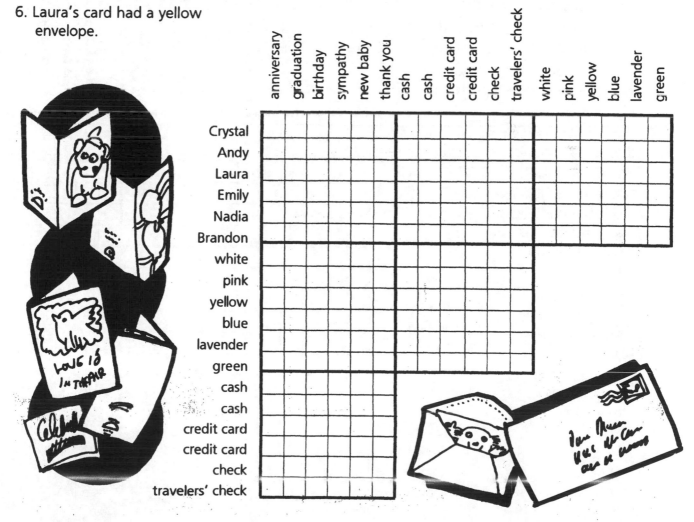

Great River Road

Each fall Jack, Muriel, Scott, Betty, Bob and Wendy enjoy driving up the Great River Road along the Mississippi. Each one enjoys photographing a different thing on the trip and looks forward to a certain segment of the excursion. Each person also has a favorite eating place along the way. Search for landmarks among these clues to determine who enjoyed doing what.

Clues

1. Jack, his wife who photographs the bluffs, his grandson who is thrilled by the Piasa Bird, his daughter who loves to eat at the old French inn, the man who could spend hours at the overlook, and the girl who loves to explore the shrine all look forward to the brilliant fall foliage.

2. Scott, his mom who admires the Lewis and Clark Memorial, his dad who enjoys the overlook, his grandpa with an eye for migrating geese, his grandma who loves to pick apples, and Wendy take turns catching the beautiful scenery on film.

3. The woman who likes to stop at the village cafe, the man who likes to picnic, the boy who loves the Burger Barn, the woman who opts for the French inn, the man who enjoys the menu at the Italian restaurant, and Wendy all enjoy the culinary stops during this trek.

4. Wendy and Jack are not related.

5. Betty is Muriel's daughter and Scott's mother.

6. Jack is the only person who would recognize wild plants in the woods.

7. The woman who enjoys the village cafe also loves to pick apples.

8. Bob does not like to picnic but does like to watch the barges passing through the locks.

9. Wendy always wants to hike the trails in the state park.

10. The boy who loves the Piasa Bird always look forward to a ride on a ferry.

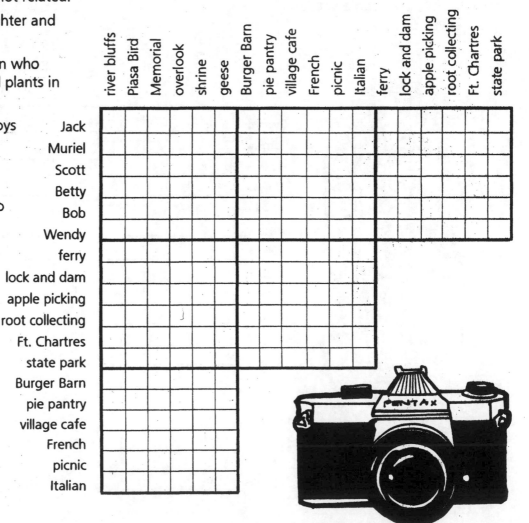

© Taylor & Francis Groups • *Logic Safari, Book 3*

Balloon Races

Tyler, Jason, Meredith, Patricia, William, Jonathan, Brian, Joe and Clay just took part in a hot-air balloon race. Their balloons were different colors, and they finished the race in 1st through 9th place. Float through these clues to determine who rode in the basket of which balloon and in what order they finished the race.

Clues

1. The balloon Tyler was in landed ahead of the green, the black, the red, the orange, the aqua, and the violet balloons but after Clay and Meredith.

2. William landed before Jason and Patricia but after Joe, Brian, Jonathan, Clay, the girl in the yellow balloon and the boy in the pink balloon.

3. Jason finished ahead of the girl in the violet balloon.

4. Brian finished before Patricia, Jason, Jonathan, and the boy in the green balloon but after Meredith, Tyler, Clay and the boy in the aqua balloon.

5. The orange balloon touched down fifth.

6. The yellow balloon finished ahead of the blue balloon.

7. The black balloon finished ahead of the red balloon.

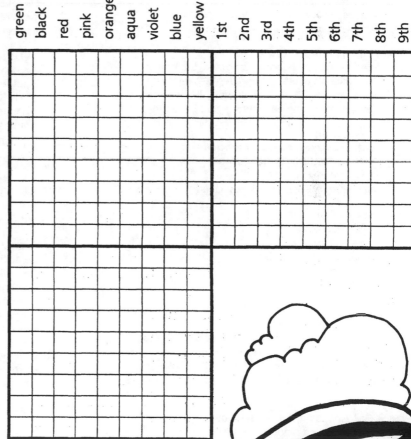

Answers

1. Yearbook, pg. 4
Marilyn - sales, Feb. 15
Linda - captions, Feb. 1
Elizabeth - layout, Jan. 20
Jonah - photography, Dec. 20

2. Camp Out, pg. 5
Cole - foil-fried potatoes, poison ivy
John - berry cobbler, briar scratches
Lance - grilled trout, sunburn
Jay - corn on the cob, chiggers

3. Miniature Golf, pg. 6
Kate - waterfall, 82
Travis - kangaroo, 80
Sandra - windmill, 75
Rich - castle, 72

4. Parent Volunteers, pg. 7
Mrs. Shields - Ed, nurse's helper, Thursday
Mr. Costello - Rachel, art appreciation, Friday
Mrs. Maxwell - Terrence, library, Tuesday
Mrs. Hoehn - Drew, math tutor, Monday

5. Lemonade Stand, pg. 8
Alex - cherries, table, make change
Zack - ice, coolers, make signs
Manuel - lemons, pitchers, wash glasses
Anna - sugar, glasses, serve customers

6. Homecoming Parade, pg. 9
Martin - bicycle brigade, 12th grade, 5th entry
Peg - queen's court, 10th grade, 12th entry
Frank - football float, 11th grade, 6th entry
Yvonne - marching band, 9th grade, 2nd entry

7. Fish Fry, pg. 10
Jane - bass, hush puppies, tablecloths
Amanda - catfish, potatoes, plates
Blake - trout, cole slaw, kettles
Sue - bluegill, apple dumplings, chairs

8. Animal Crackers, pg. 11
Chad - bears, 36
Christina - fish, 38
Cassandra - chickens, 32
Sam - lions, 24
Christopher - cows, 42
Molly - elephants, 28

9. Trivia Contest, pg. 12
Forrest - 6th grade, history, 325 points, 40 pledges
Debra - 8th grade, movies, 380 points, 25 pledges
Gene - 7th grade, sports, 368 points, 45 pledges
Vicky - 8th grade, television, 392 points, 30 pledges

10. Apple Orchard, pg. 13
Gail - Jonathan, 11/2 bushels, third, apple cider
Eric - golden delicious, 1 bushel, first, apple cider
Tami - red delicious, 3 pecks, second, apple butter
Greg - winesap, 2 pecks, fourth, apple pie

11. Copy Cats, pg. 14
Kate - Betsy Ross, 10
Carlos - Abraham Lincoln, 8
Jack - Thomas Jefferson, 9
Craig - John Hancock, 7
Neal - Ben Franklin, 4
Daniel - George Washington, 5

12. Team Pictures, pg. 15
Kevin - Olson. Tornadoes, blue, 1:15
Jeff - Tate, Cardinals, red, 1:45
Doug - Reynolds, Bobcats, gray, 1:00
Paul - Hersey, Cougars, maroon, 12:30

13. Natural Disaster Kits, pg. 16
Mr. Smith - radios, 5th
Mrs. Wilson - distilled water, 4th
Mr. Hiatt - first aid supplies, 3rd
Mrs. Althoff - flashlights, 2nd
Mr. Detwiler - food, 6th
Mrs. Horowitz - batteries, 1st

14. Student of the Week, pg. 17
Justin Adams - Mrs. Maloney, bumper sticker, 1st week of Oct.
Maria Sousa - Mrs. Kinney, certificate, 1st week of Dec.
Nicholas Barton - Mrs. Horstmann, lunch with principal, 3rd week of Oct.
Danielle Chang - Mrs. Buck, button, 2nd week of Feb.

15. Tyler's Birthday, pg. 18
Grandma and Grandpa - push glowworm, potato salad
Aunt Amy - bubble machine, deviled eggs
Uncle Randy - foam bat and ball, vegetable tray
Aunt Bonnie - squeeze light-up toy, gelatin salad
Cousin Becky - sidewalk chalk, barbecued meat
Mom and Dad - rocking horse, birthday cake

16. Water Balloon Fight, pg. 19
Andrew - Todd, patio table, blue, 35
Brent - Casey, front porch, orange, 38
Matt - Jose, wheelbarrow, yellow, 40
Ted - Miguel, garden, red, 34

17. Family Garden, pg. 20
Great Grandma Frona - roses, cuttings
Great Grandma Pearl - irises, rhizomes
Grandma Maxine - poppies, seeds
Grandma Mary - tiger lilies, bulbs
Grandpa Jack - peonies, roots
Great Aunt Kitty - hollyhocks, seeds

18. Golf Lessons, pg. 21
Joseph - putting, 2:15, Lee, Deer Meadows
Roberto - chipping, 1:30, Lee, Deer Meadows
Rick - sand traps, 10:30, Beaver Creek, Charlie
Jenny - driving, 12:00, Beaver Creek, Charlie

19. Pine Wood Derby, pg. 22
Robby - den 7, blue ribbon, 10:00, Mrs. Bishop
Adam - den 2, silver, 12:15, Mrs. Liming
Mike - den 4, bronze, 11:30, Mrs. Barnes
Nathan - den 9, gold, 12:45, Mrs. Rose

20. Secretaries Day, pg. 23
Gwen - Dr. Waite, flowers, Mexican, medical
Nate - Dr. Yoshioka, macadamia nuts, seafood, weight counseling
Geneva - Ms. Drewes, flowers, vegetarian, real estate
Karen - Mr. Risby, chocolates, Italian, insurance

21. Kittens, pg. 24
Boots - calico, ribbon, male, basket, middle
Bear - orange, mouse, male, recliner, youngest
Suzy - black and white, ball, female, kitchen chair, middle
Sugar - white, yarn ball, female, daybed, oldest

22. Garage Sale, pg. 25
Peter - baseball cars, green, $36.00
Cindy - books and posters, yellow, $35.00
David - sports equipment, blue, $42.00
Jane - clothes, white, $31.00
Kathy - toys, pink, $28.50

23. Mothers' Day, pg. 26
Heather - Mrs. Wingrove, bouquet, breakfast in bed
Jessica - Mrs. Deutsch, card, massage
Joanne - Mrs. Yamada, rose bush, dinner
April - Mrs. Avery, bath salts, manicure
Sherita - Mrs. Cobb, sleep shirt, concert tickets

24. April Creek Walk, pg. 27
Pamela Rubin - tadpole, morel
Vernon Ho - chipmunk, mayapple
Sean Lewandowski - garter snake, fern
Tiffany O'Brien - tree frog, buttercup
Shana Walker - box turtle, trillium

25. School Carnival, pg. 28
Leah - ring toss, 9:30-10:30, Mr. Gonzalez
Kenneth - face painting, 10:30-11:30, Mrs. Fishman
Troy - snow cones, 1:30-2.30, Mrs. Nixon
Tasha - fish pond, 12:30-1:30, Mrs. Hollinger
Darren - hot dogs, 8:30-9:30, Mr. Lomax
Jenna - lollipop tree, 11:30-12:30, Mr. Sarni

26. The Card Shop, pg. 29
Crystal - new baby, blue, cash
Andy - graduation, green, credit card
Laura - anniversary - yellow cash
Emily - sympathy, lavender, travelers' check
Nadia - birthday, pink, credit card
Brandon - thank you, white, check

27. Great River Road, pg. 30
Jack - geese, root gathering, picnic
Muriel - river bluffs, apples, village cafe
Scott - Piasa Bird, ferry, Burger Barn
Betty - Lewis and Clark Memorial, Fort Chartres, French inn
Bob - overlook, lock and dam, Italian restaurant
Wendy - shrine, state park, pie pantry

28. Balloon Races, pg. 31
Tyler - pink, 3rd
Jason - red, 8th
Meredith - yellow, 1st
Patricia - violet, 9th
William - green, 7th
Jonathan - black, 6th
Brian - orange, 5th
Joe - aqua, 4th
Clay - blue, 2nd

Common Core State Standards Alignment Sheet
Logic Safari (Book 3)

All lessons in this book align to the following standards.

Grade Level	Common Core State Standards in ELA-Literacy
Grade 5	RF.5.3 Know and apply grade-level phonics and word analysis skills in decoding words. RF.5.4 Read with sufficient accuracy and fluency to support comprehension.